To my darling Chins,
With millions of love on our
43rd Wedding Anniversary and always.
Dany
xxxx
xxx

CW00666373

August 27th 2009

PORTRAIT OF
THE GALLOWAY
COASTLINE

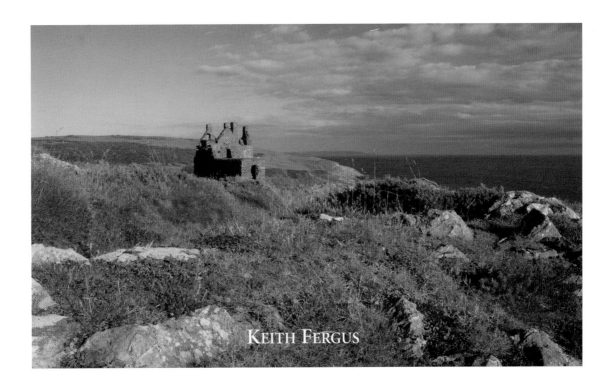

KEITH FERGUS

HALSGROVE

First published in Great Britain in 2009

Copyright © Keith Fergus 2009

All rights reserved. No part of this publication may be reproduced,
stored in a retrieval system, or transmitted in any form or by any
means without the prior permission of the copyright holder.

British Library Cataloguing-in-Publication Data
A CIP record for this title is available from the British Library

ISBN 978 1 84114 926 4

HALSGROVE
Halsgrove House,
Ryelands Industrial Estate,
Bagley Road, Wellington, Somerset TA21 9PZ
Tel: 01823 653777   Fax: 01823 216796
email: sales@halsgrove.com

Part of the Halsgrove group of companies
Information on all Halsgrove titles is available at: www.halsgrove.com

Printed and bound by Grafiche Flaminia, Italy

Acknowledgements

The Galloway coastline has played a major part in my life, and some of my happiest times have been spent here, and many more I hope are still to come. Therefore, I am indebted to my parents for the holidays we spent here. They have since settled near the Galloway coast and as a result my visits to this wonderful region have become even more frequent, and never without my camera. And so, this book would never have happened without them, and I can only thank them for that.

I must also thank my wife, Helen, and my two beautiful children, Kyla and Cameron, for their continued support and patience as I wait for the next moment to click the shutter, although they too may not have got to enjoy Galloway in all its glory without my need to photograph it – that is my excuse anyway!!

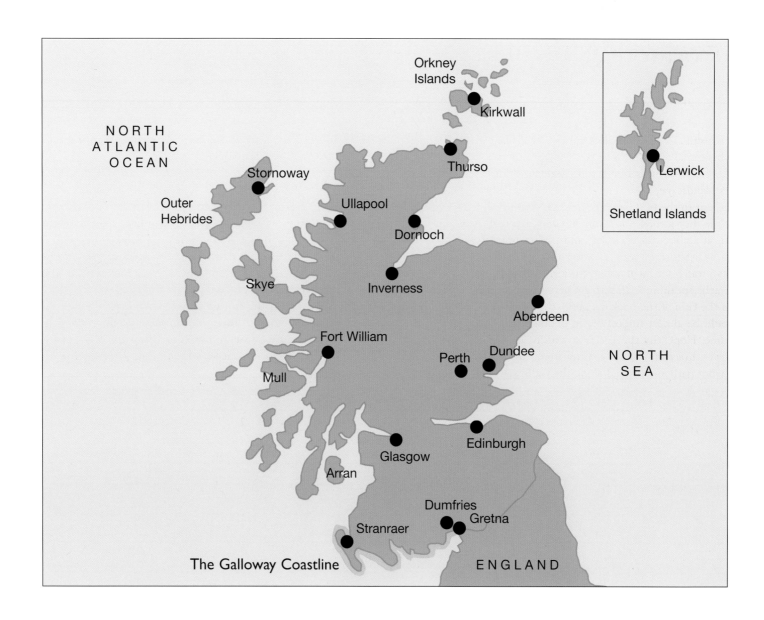

Introduction

As people follow the great trunk road of the M74 north and south, many will be unaware of the astonishing stretch of coastline that begins a couple of miles west of the motorway, one which is on a par with anything else Scotland has to offer.

The Galloway coastline begins near the village of Gretna and then twists and turns its way south and westwards across a remarkably diverse landscape, one which takes you past some beautiful villages, idyllic beaches, coves, cliffs and mountains, all of them adding an ingredient to the flavour of this corner of Scotland, before reaching its (and Scotland's) most southerly point at the Mull of Galloway. The coastline then strikes north into a wilder, remoter landscape which, for these very reasons, is equally rewarding as what has gone before – the lighthouses, castles, ports, and place-names testament to the history embedded in the region. Once Milleur Point is reached, the coastline heads south into Loch Ryan and towards the major ports of Stranraer and Cairnryan. Loch Ryan is a natural harbour and from here you can watch (or take) one of the ferries which journey daily to and fro from Ireland, a country indelibly linked with Galloway as it was the Gaelic speaking Irish settling here which gave rise to the name Galloway, 'Land of the Foreign Gael'.

As the title of the book suggests, the photographs displayed are a representation of what this fantastic stretch of coastline has to offer. It would be almost impossible to photograph every single nook and cranny, and I have tried to cover and illustrate the diversity of the coastline. Hopefully the selection within these pages conveys this. I also hope the next time you are travelling along the M74, or from whatever direction you are coming from, this book of photographs will instil some wandering spirit in you, and take you away from the well worn path and instead along the Galloway coast.

Keith Fergus

The Galloway coastline has an inauspicious beginning, as here stormy clouds zip across the sky looking back over great mud banks towards Gretna.

However, beautiful colours lie along the shoreline…   as well as in lichen coloured rocks…

and a wonderful array of coloured stones.

Annan has many wonderful buildings along its high street
including the Old Parish Church.

Left:
Salmon stakes (seen here near Annan) are also a regular occurrence along the
coastline. England lies only a couple of miles from here across the channel.

The wonderful and imposing Annan Town Hall is the focal
point of Annan's high street. It was built in 1878 with the
magnificent clock tower as its centrepiece.

Right:
The railway bridge at Annan spans the width of the River Annan as
it makes its way to the Solway Firth only a mile or so down river.

A magnificent sunrise over the Solway Firth from Powfoot. This idyllic spot was purpose-built as a holiday village at the turn of the twentieth century and it is still a popular destination for visitors to the Galloway coast.

Powfoot also offers magnificent views of the great mountains of the Lake District.

The profile of Criffel dominates the initial stretches of the coastline
and is first seen from the shoreline near Queensberry.

Right:
The orange glow of dawn is reflected in the Solway Firth near Queensberry.

Ruthwell Church houses Ruthwell Cross, one of the most significant examples of Anglo Saxon stonework which dates back to 680AD. The cross was moved to Ruthwell Church in 1887.

A low winter's mist hangs over the Solway Firth at Caerlaverock, the sun trying its best to sneak through.

The dramatic remains of Caerlaverock Castle, a thirteenth-century triangular moated castle, lie a few miles from Dumfries. Because of its close proximity to the English border, it has had to defend itself many times over the centuries. The castle was permanently abandoned in 1640, and is now under ownership of Historic Scotland and is a popular tourist attraction.

Left:
Caerlaverock Nature Reserve is a haven for many types of birds, including barnacle geese, whooper swans and oystercatchers, seen here searching for food at dawn.

Criffel reflected in the River Urr at dawn near Caerlaverock.

Right:
The Solway Firth provides dramatic reflections at sunset over Criffel.

The River Nith reaches the Solway Firth as it flows from Dumfries towards Glencaple. The sandy soils are perfect for many wildflowers as summer approaches. Glencaple used to be a busy port with ships regularly sailing from here to the Americas and the West Indies.

A haaf netter catches a fish at Glencaple.

Two haaf netters wait patiently for their catch to enter their nets, standing still for many hours at a time in the estuary. Haaf netting was introduced by the Vikings, the word haaf meaning 'sea net'.

Three cows making the most of the Solway Firth's low tide near Glencaple. The Solway Firth translates as 'Firth of the Muddy Ford', the meaning self-evident here.

The Devorgilla Bridge which spans the River Nith at Dumfries, is one of Scotland's oldest bridges still in use. It was built in 1432.

Left:
Dumfries, seen here at night, was founded as a Royal Burgh in 1186 and lies on the banks of the River Nith, a tidal river which flows directly into the Solway Firth. Robert the Bruce murdered the Red (John) Comyn in nearby Greyfriars Kirk whilst Robert Burns spent the final few years of his life in the town, dying here in 1796.

The Robert Burns Centre, Dumfries.

Mist clings to the Urr Valley at sunrise.

The humble beginnings of an oak tree begin
at ground level in Shambellie Wood.

Left:
The beautiful array of autumn colours
on display at Shambellie Wood.

Located near New Abbey, Shambellie Wood offers some of the finest autumn colours to be seen along the Galloway coast. Shambellie House is also home to the National Museum of Costume.

The wonderful remains of Sweetheart Abbey can be found at New Abbey. This late thirteenth/early fourteenth-century Cistercian abbey was founded by Devorgilla, Lady of Galloway, in memory of her husband, John Balliol.

The great bulk of Criffel rises behind Sweetheart Abbey.

John Paul Jones' cottage near Arbigland. Jones is possibly more famous in the United States than he is in his homeland as he is the founding father of the American Navy. He was born near Kirkbean in 1747.

Left:
Late winter sunshine beautifully highlights the great ridges and contours of the Lake District mountains, lying a few miles across the Solway Firth, from here at Carsethorn.

The small scattering of houses at Southerness, seen here at dawn with Southerness lighthouse on the left.

Hay bales at the foot of Criffel at dawn near Southerness.

Left:
Southerness Lighthouse is one of the oldest in Scotland. It was built as a marker in 1749 to ensure safe passage for ships through the Nith estuary with a light being added in about 1800. The light was extinguished in the 1930s. The lighthouse is now a tourist attraction.

The remains of Wreath Tower near Southerness, thought to date from the sixteenth century.

Sand dunes near Mersehead with the Colvend coast on the horizon emphasising
the great diversity that the Galloway coastline has to offer.

Field mouse ear.

Right:
Looking along the Colvend coast from the small hamlet of Mainsriddle.

Much of the Galloway coastline is subject to very high and very low tides. Here at Sandyhills, the water-filled channels left at low tide beautifully reflect the warm colours of sunrise. However, the low tides make the immediate area susceptible to quicksand.

Climbing from Sandyhills, a path takes you high onto the cliffs which offer spectacular views along the coast.

The tiny hamlet of Portling sits slightly off the beaten track and does not see many visitors. Its beach is one of the most pleasant along this stretch of coastline with great views of the cliffs and coast. You can walk all the way along the coast from Sandyhills to Kippford without hitting tarmac, and Portling is one of the many scenic highpoints along the way.

Left:
The cliffs above Sandyhills climb to The Torrs giving wonderful views along the Colvend coast, particularly at dawn. The scattering of houses below The Torrs is Portling.

The charming remains of an old cottage near Portling.

Another spectacular vantage point along the Colvend coast cliff path is the one from Barcloy Hill. Here, the setting sun hits the whitewashed houses of Rockcliffe.

The Galloway coastline is often witness to some spectacular sunsets, with this one over Hestan from Castle Point being a case in point.

A site of great historical importance is Castle Point near Rockcliffe. The remains of an Iron Age fort dating from 200AD lie here, and some of the original ditches and stonework are still visible. Commanding views to the east and south would have identified Castle Point as an important defensive site and steep cliffs on three sides in addition to its position would certainly have made it problematic to any would-be attackers.

The Solway Firth, Rough Island and Screel at dusk from Castle Point.

Hestan Island at dusk.

The sun sets in dramatic fashion behind Screel from Rockcliffe.

Left:
Hestan Island, seen here from Rockcliffe, was the inspiration for Samuel Rutherford
Crocket's famous novel *The Raiders*. At certain times when there is a very
low tide, Hestan is accessible on foot using a natural shingle causeway and is
worth a visit. There is a lighthouse on the island which was built in 1850.

Rockcliffe is a haven for tourists, and has been since Victorian times when many of its seafront houses were built allowing for some tremendous views of Hestan and the bird sanctuary of Rough Island.

Looking across Rough Island to Hestan and Castle Point from Mote of Mark. Not surprisingly, given its position, the Mote of Mark was once a defended hilltop and was supposedly a court of a mighty Dark Age chieftain. The site was certainly occupied in the sixth century but destroyed by fire in the seventh, with excavations over the years finding the remains of a timber hut, imported jewellery, metalwork and glassware. These days, the Mote of Mark is a place to sit and simply take in the wonderful views.

Castle Point at dawn from Rough Island.

Looking along the Urr estuary from Rough Island at dawn. Rough Island is a bird sanctuary and has been under ownership of the National Trust of Scotland since 1937. Again, at low tide it is accessible on foot although, due to nesting, the island should be avoided during the months of May and June.

A tremendous carpet of
bluebells on the Jubilee
Path near Rockcliffe.

Mark Hill (or The Muckle as it is known locally) offers an astounding vantage point to look along the Galloway coastline. Here, Rough Island and Castle Point lie below with the Cumbrian mountains visible on the distant horizon.

The Colvend coast at dusk from the coastal path near Kippford.

Left:
In the opposite direction, The Muckle presents a tremendous view
along the Urr estuary, with yachts at Kippford lying below.

A single boat lit by the evening sun with Rough Island in the distance.

Beautiful colours and textures adorn this old dinghy.

Kippford is now an important centre for yachting but in its heyday was a significant
coastal port with small sloops being built on the shore with 350–400 tonne ships frequently
visiting the pier. Here the setting sun highlights the buildings which line the seafront.

A fantastic array of colours is reflected in the River Urr at Kippford
as the sun sets behind the twin peaks of Screel and Bengairn.

Orcharton Tower near Palnackie, is Scotland's only cylindrical tower.

A seat provides welcome relief for the walker attempting to climb to
the top of Screel and another fabulous point to view the coastline.

Balcary Tower is a nineteenth-century fortified tower and sits proudly on a promontory at Balcary Bay. A small fishing trawler awaits the incoming tide.

The unmistakeable profiles of the great Lake District mountains are beautifully
silhouetted against the rising sun, seen here from Balcary Bay.

A good path leaves Balcary Bay, climbs high onto the cliffs above the sea,
and provides an exciting, if at times exposed, walk to Rascarrel Bay.

Balcary Point presents a view of Hestan's dramatic profile. The pink tones of thrift provide a splash of colour at dusk.

Kirkcudbright is still very much a fishing village with trawlers coming and going on a daily basis. Kirkcudbright means 'The Kirk of St Cuthbert' and was named after the saint. The town was established as a Royal Burgh in 1455.

Kirkcudbright is now a popular tourist destination and heralds itself as 'The Artists Town' due to the number of painters and craft workers who live and work there.

Looking across to Little Ross Lighthouse from Kirkcudbright Bay.

The fantastic colours and textures of an old fishing trawler near
Ross Bay are accentuated by the late winter sunshine.

Right:
Strong winds whip up the waters around the Sound of Ross
with Little Ross Lighthouse standing firm against the elements.

Common scurvy grass.

Left:
Little Ross Lighthouse was built in 1843 by the engineer Alan Stevenson.
He was also responsible for some of Scotland's most celebrated lighthouses
including the ones at Ardnamurchan, Skerryvore, and Chanonry Point.

Storm clouds gather over the low-lying Fleet Islands as seen from Carrick.

A shag stretches its wings on a warm, sunny morning near Carrick.

Wintry showers sweep across Fleet Bay at dawn from Sandgreen.

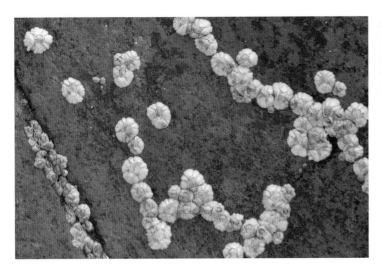

A necklace of limpets cling to the rocks along the coastline.

Right:
Shells at Sandgreen are highlighted by the low-lying
winter sun. Sandgreen is home to a scattering of
houses and a small caravan park and due to its out
of the way location is a peaceful haven of tranquillity.

Looking across Fleet Bay from Mossyard.

A great bank of cloud high above the Fleet Islands beautifully echoes the line of a drystone dyke above Mossyard.

The Belted Galloway, which has become synonymous with the region, is a rare breed of beef cattle ideally suited to living on the moorland of Galloway. They possess a double coat, one of long hair which sheds the rain and a soft undercoat for warmth.

Right:
The magnificent remains of Cardoness Castle overlooks Fleet Bay on the outskirts of Gatehouse of Fleet. The castle was built by the McCullochs in the fifteenth century who were regularly in conflict with their neighbours. Cardoness Castle was deserted in the seventeenth century after Sir Godfrey McCulloch's execution following the murder of William Gordon of Buck. The castle is now under ownership of Historic Scotland and is a tourist attraction.

Situated above and overlooking Wigtown Bay lies Cairnholy, two chambered cairns (this one is Cairnholy 1) which in the past were used for ritual ceremonies. The site was excavated in 1949, although little is known about any burials which took place here due to the acidic nature of the soil dissolving any remains.

The remains of old salmon stake nets near Creetown at sunset.

Adamson Square, Creetown, with its wonderful contemporary granite sculpture sitting below the old clock tower.

Bluebell.

Damselfly.

A cloud inversion cloaks the Solway Firth with the mountains of the Lake District peeking over the horizon.

Cairnsmore of Fleet at 711 metres is the highest point of the Galloway coastline and offers exceptional views along its length.

A lone walker enjoys the tremendous vantage point from near the summit of Cairnsmore of Fleet with the rolling hills of Galloway and Ayrshire on show.

Right:
The whaleback ridge of Cairnsmore of Fleet from near Wigtown, Scotland's National Book Town.

Autumn colours line the River Bladnoch as it makes its journey towards the Cree estuary at Wigtown Bay.

Oystercatchers at low tide, Garlieston.

Fishing boat, Garlieston.

Dusk over Wigtown Bay from Portyerrock.

Hay bales, Isle of Whithorn.

Colourful houses line the main street of the Isle of Whithorn, a small fishing village near the southern point of The Machars. The village is no longer an isle as a causeway was built in 1790 to improve links with the mainland.

Stormy skies at dusk, Isle of Whithorn. In the 1800s, the Isle had strong links with both Ireland and the Isle of Man. The harbour is still the main focal point of the village with boats bringing in their catches of crabs, lobsters and scallops.

The dramatic coastline of the Isle of Whithorn with St Ninian's Chapel to the left. St Ninian, who is acknowledged at Scotland's first saint and missionary, built his first church in nearby Whithorn.

Some believe that the Isle of Whithorn was the first port of call when St Ninian arrived in Scotland whilst it has also been intimated that St Ninian's Chapel is the site of St Ninian's original church. The Isle of Man lies only 18 miles away on the horizon.

The most probable explanation for the chapel is that it was used by the many pilgrims who came by sea to visit St Ninian's church at Whithorn.

As the coastline turns west, the cliffs rise at Burrow Head with wildflowers in
abundance as you walk along the coast, like these lovely sea campion.

Looking along spectacular cliffs towards Burrow Head.

Left:
A small fishing trawler working away at dusk near Burrow Head. On the horizon lies the Mull of Galloway, Scotland's most southerly point.

The setting sun highlights the beautiful, rounded stones at Port Castle Bay, with St Ninian's Cave set into the cliffs behind. It has been said that the cave was used by St Ninian as a place of solitude and many Christian symbols were recovered during excavations in the last century.

Left:
Stone detail, Port Castle Bay.

Gavin Maxwell Memorial near Monreith. Gavin Maxwell was the author of the highly influential and successful *Ring of Bright Water*. He was born a few miles away in Elrig.

A seagull finds a perch near Point of Lag.

The appropriately named Point of Lag, a spectacular setting for St Medan's golf course, the most southerly course in Scotland.

Old fence above Monreith Bay.

The almost perfect semicircle of Monreith Bay stretching all the way to Barshalloch Point.

The receding tide leave ripples in the sand at Port William,
the pattern highlighted by the low winter sun.

Right:
Stone detail, Port William.

Auchenmalg Bay.

Left:
The boulder-strewn beach near Barr Point allows for
fantastic views along the quiet inlet of Auchenmalg Bay.

The spectacular remains of Glenluce Abbey, a twelfth-century Cistercian Abbey which was built in 1190 by Roland, Lord of Galloway. It is now under the care of Historic Scotland and is a popular tourist attraction.

Storm clouds move in over Luce Bay. The coastline leaves the Machars and moves into the Rhins of Galloway.

A winter's dawn over Sandhead, the clouds perfectly reflected in one of the many pools at low tide.

Drummore has the distinction of being Scotland's most southerly village, lying a few miles from the Mull of Galloway. Due to the close proximity of the Rhinns of Galloway to Ireland, many of the place names have their origins associated with Gaelic. Galloway itself translates as 'Land of the Foreign Gael' whilst Drummore means 'big ridge'.

Once you leave Drummore the final few miles to the Mull of Galloway are spectacular,
a single track road leading to the lighthouse, great cliffs and wonderful views.

Once you reach the road end you can drive no further. A short walk will take you to the wonderful Mull of Galloway Lighthouse. It was built in 1830 by Robert Stevenson, one of the many noted lighthouse engineers of the Stevenson family. The position of the lighthouse offers, on a clear day, views of the Isle of Man and Ireland as well as much of the Galloway coastline.

An old cottage has been renovated into an excellent
visitor centre at Mull of Galloway.

Left:
The lighthouse cost £9000 to complete, is 85 feet in
height and stands atop vertical cliffs standing approximately
260 feet above the sea. The light was converted to electricity in
1971 and the lighthouse was fully automated in 1988.

There is only a scattering of cottages punctuating the landscape around the Mull.
Because of the Gulf Stream, the weather can be clement with snow or frost being a rarity.

The rocks to the left of the picture are the Gallie Craig,
officially Scotland's most southerly point.

A yacht awaits the incoming tide at Port Logan beside the harbour's distinctive lighthouse.

The small but beautiful village of Port Logan lying a few miles north of the Mull of Galloway. This quiet township nestles within a lovely bay and has become better known since the popular BBC series 'Two Thousand Acres of Sky' was filmed here.

The renowned Logan Botanic Gardens near Port Logan. Again, because of the warm Gulf Stream air, an exotic range of plants flourishes in the wonderful gardens, visitors coming from far and wide to view the array of flora.

Beautiful colours, Logan Botanic Gardens.

The rocks and cliffs near Dunskey provide an ideal perch for seagulls.

Left:
Dunskey Castle lies a short walk along the cliff top from Portpatrick
and occupies a dramatic position which provides a fantastic vantage point
to view the Rhinns coastline and across to Ireland. The castle was built
in the sixteenth century for the Adairs of Kinhilt.

The first rays of dawn hit the small village of Portpatrick. The village was named after St Patrick who used the port when making the short trip across the sea from Ireland. Portpatrick is also the beginning of the Southern Upland Way, which at 212 miles is Scotland's longest long distance path.

The lovely front of Portpatrick at dusk.

A monumental sky approaches Portpatrick. The lighthouse on the left was built in 1893.

Fishing trawler, Portpatrick.

Right:
The lovely harbour at Portpatrick is
home to many yachts and fishing vessels.

Looking towards the lovely bays of Port Mora and Port Kale from the Southern Upland Way.

The magnificent Killantringan Lighthouse sitting on Black Head near Killantringan Bay. The lighthouse was built by David Stevenson in 1900. It stands 72 feet in height and was automated in 1988.

Strong winds are part and parcel of living on the west coast, and it is no different here as waves crash into shore at the dramatic Killantringan Bay.

A ferry passes Corsewall Lighthouse on its way to Ireland. The lighthouse stands above Corsewall Point and was built by the famous engineer Robert Stevenson. The lighthouse is now a hotel.

The northern coastline of
Galloway near Corsewall Point is
a wild place and sparsely
populated, much of the land
being used for agriculture.

Looking across Milleur Point
(the northernmost tip
of Galloway) along the
Ayrshire coastline from
Balshalloch above Loch Ryan.

Loch Ryan is a sea loch and as it is surrounded by land on three sides it acts as a natural
harbour for the major town of Stranraer and the village of Cairnryan amongst others.

Fishing boats, Stranraer harbour. There has been a harbour at Stranraer since the eighteenth century.

Stranraer and Loch Ryan. Stranraer is the largest settlement and the gateway to the Rhinns of Galloway. It is also the largest settlement in Southwest Scotland and the main ferry port for ferries running between Scotland and Northern Ireland.

The Galloway coastline nears its end a few miles north of Cairnryan. The lighthouse stands near the entrance of Loch Ryan. In the 1970s, P&O decided upon Cairnryan as the location for its roll-on-roll-off ferry terminus which offered a shorter crossing to Larne.

Stena Line intend to move their services from Stranraer to Cairnryan in the coming years.

The ferry leaves Loch Ryan and Galloway en route to Ireland.